BECOME THE CONSCIOUS FUTURIST THE WORLD NEEDS NOW

An Introduction to Conscious Futures

Charlotte Kemp

Futures Alchemy Publishers

Dedication

The global pandemic that started in 2020 has affected everyone in some way. The world is not turning out the way we expected it to.

Some of the most hardest hit people are those in the events industry. When coming together in large groups, the staple of live events, is forbidden by law across the world, it is difficult to find a way to continue to exist.

This book is dedicated to the incredible people in the South African Events Council, who week after week came together to support each other, share research, write safety protocols, support the industry, uphold the law while still trying to support their own association members, keep their own businesses afloat and their staff employed.

*I am privileged to have served along side them.
They have my utmost respect.*

Contents

Preface

This introduction to being a Conscious Futurist is only the start of the journey. It may seem a naive model in the face of real world problems, but as someone who has moved up and down this spiral a few times, I find it helpful as a reminder that in any dark time, there is a time after this time, and a way to move back up the Spiral.

The story in Chapter 5, of Alex and her challenges, is a fictional story compiled of many stories, accounts and experiences. It is meant only as an illustration of how the Spiral can work.

#1 Introduction

It's time for a little philosophy.

Although we will be exploring some new ideas, the concept of being a Conscious Futurist isn't intended to present you with a tonne of new tools or models to apply to your life or your work. Being a Conscious Futurist is a lens through which you see life. It is a mindset, a philosophical framework for you to use as a platform to do the work that you do, to create your art, to express your life.

Regardless of what your occupation is or what it says on your business card or your CV, I want you to also think of yourself in two new ways.

You are a Philosopher

A philosopher looks at the fundamental nature of existence and the reasons why we value certain things, or act in certain ways. Philosophers take time to consider life as opposed to rushing through each day only reacting to stimulus. Philosophers consider.

If you spend any time in personal or professional development, if you read widely or listen to podcasts or spend time exploring new ideas, then you are a philosopher. You may not have the ancient Greek robes. You may not be sitting on the top of a mountain or meditating beneath a tree. But you are considering. Contemplating. Wondering. Playing with ideas in your mind about how things might be and why they might be that way. And where they might be going in the future. Which means that you are something in addition to being a philosopher.

You are also a Futurist

I believe that everyone is a futurist. If you have ever wondered about your future, if you have saved towards your retirement, if you have children and planned for their education or wondered about their careers, if you have made plans for a holiday or built a house or proposed marriage, or run a business, then you are a futurist. We are all natural futurists. But we could be better futurists. We can learn some of the skills and models that will help us contemplate these issues with better data and better results.

And we can also become Conscious Futurists

A Conscious Futurist isn't only aware of the future but makes informed and sometimes difficult decisions to act according to their conscience, in order to produce better results for more than just themselves. They act in a way that brings more value into the world than they take out of it.

Why do we need to be philosophical conscious futurists?

We need to ask the questions that other people aren't asking. And we need to do that because most of the world is pretty unconscious, about, well, everything that is going on.

They have their priorities, they have their 'to-do 'lists, they are aware of the pressures, demands, deadlines, and those things that are urgent and pressing on them. But beyond that, they tend to go through the world pretty much unconsciously, using a system of habits to get through each day.

Sometimes something happens to interrupt that pattern. It could be an illness, a marriage, or a birthday ending with a zero. Or a year like 2020. But something happens to shake people out of their comfortable illusion that everything is ticking along and acceptable. Something happens that makes people experience the trauma of being thrust into philosophical mode without any preparation. We normally call it a 'mid-life crisis', or these days even a 'quarter-life crisis'. Many people try to shake it off or suppress the difficult and uncomfortable questions with the purchase of a new car or a new spouse. But if you are the philosophical, conscious futurist who ends up reading this book, then it is because you want to explore those questions that other people tend to avoid.

The pandemic that started in 2020 gave us pause to reflect. We had to pause because it was the law! We needed to start thinking about things more, a lot more. Why are we doing what we are doing? What do we miss from the past? What are we going to miss in the future? Do we want to set everything back the way it was? Are there choices, behaviours, values, goals that we inherited rather than those that we intentionally chose? Perhaps the past wasn't as good as we imagined and we would be doing ourselves a huge disservice to try to go back to it.

We want to interrupt the unconscious ways that we operate and experience our world first hand. We need to find new, intentional, conscious ways of showing up.

#2 Why This Book And This Topic?

Have you ever driven home from work, or on a regular route, found yourself at your destination, and then wondered how you got there, with no memory of the road, or making decisions at traffic lights. Perhaps you experienced, as I do when this happens, a momentary panic that you may have done something wrong on the road without even being aware of it.

And what about those birthdays that end in a zero. Thirty. Forty! Fifty!! Let's not go further. Anniversaries, New Year's Eves, and other calendar milestones are all fraught with anxiety about the quality of our lives. We start to ask deep philosophical questions like, why am I here? What am I doing with my life? Who would notice if I disappeared tomorrow? Have I sacrificed my dreams? What legacy am I leaving? Can I afford cosmetic surgery to get rid of these wrinkles?

These are all signs that we sometimes move through life unconsciously. We get stuck in a routine that we have designed for an efficient life, and then we let the routine determine our lives instead of adjusting the routine to fit our aspirations. If we are obeying our diaries instead of shaping our diaries with our goals, then we may be slipping into an unconscious way of living.

Let us be honest. You cannot be fully conscious all the time of the entire miracle of life. You cannot make every decision into an opportunity for deep, thoughtful reflection. You need to be able to make some decisions by remote control and you need to be able to take some parts of your life for granted, at least for part of the time. If we didn't have routines and habits and assumptions then we could never get from dawn to sundown in an efficient way. But we cannot let those routines, habits, and assumptions control us.

Change how you think about yourself

So how then do we avoid overreactions? How do we ensure that our next big birthday isn't a time of turmoil and regret?

Change how you think about yourself. Try this on for size. You are a creative, conscious being, with agency over your own future and it is a future that you have reflected on and intentionally designed. Does that sound like a life worth exploring?

The danger of unconscious philosophy

We should not allow ourselves to slip into philosophical reflection without a few precautions. Unexperienced philosophers run the risk of over reaction. When people discover at age 50, that their lives are not fulfilling or that they have abandoned a long-forgotten, teenage ambition, they sometimes respond by rejecting what they have and impulsively pursuing a new goal. Marriages end, careers are thrown over, prematurely balding men purchase sports cars and women line up for tummy tucks.

None of those things are necessarily wrong, but if we practiced a little more philosophy, a little more often, then we could design lives worth living, not wake up to a life we suddenly re-evaluate as our own, personal hell.

Experienced philosophers and futurists can continually re-evaluate their direction and make adjustments. These small course-corrections can help us to live better lives that need minor upgrades from time to time, instead of complete overhauls.

We could save a great deal of money and emotional turmoil, by spending more time in philosophical reflection.

#3 On Being Conscious

The use of the word 'conscious 'has risen dramatically in recent decades, and yet some people still feel like it is a vaguely esoteric word. So let us use the word as it is defined in the dictionary, to mean 'the state of being aware of and responsive to one's surroundings'. It is a word that is used in philosophy, of course, as well as in psychology and medicine. Someone who is unconscious in medical language is someone unable to respond to the world around them, and that leaves them completely vulnerable and at the mercy of others. This is a very practical word.

When you search online for the word 'conscious 'and then look for images, you will inevitably find pictures of stars in the sky, or of people's heads, or of people standing on mountain tops gazing up at the stars. The pictures are lovely, but they reinforce that vaguely esoteric sensation that many people have about being conscious. Let us keep it to mean that we are aware of, paying attention to, responding to, not avoiding or ignoring but really seeing and recognising what is going on.

That doesn't mean that we are going to be able to solve everything we see that is wrong in the world. This is reality after all, not a fantasy. Being conscious means that sometimes we are going to be aware of something that is wrong that we cannot resolve and we have to live with that. But at least we are not pretending to ourselves that it didn't exist. We are not oblivious and we have faced facts, sought inconvenient information, and considered it. Even if it is uncomfortable, we have been mindful and engaged.

4 Stages of Learning Model

A helpful model to consider as we begin to explore how consciousness applies to our lives is that of the 4 Stages of Learning. The origins of this model are disputed, and it can be demonstrated either as a pyramid representing a hierarchy or as a 2x2 matrix.

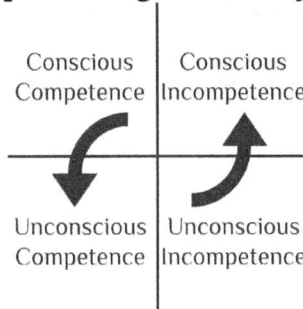

Conscious Competence	Conscious Incompetence
Unconscious Competence	Unconscious Incompetence

Unconsciously Incompetent

We start at the bottom right-hand corner where we are unconsciously incompetent. There exists something about which we have no skills or competence, but we don't even know at this point, that we don't know it.

The example that is often given to illustrate these stages, is that of driving a car. Young children who are being ferried around to school or friends 'houses aren't even aware of the fact that they don't know how to drive. They are unconsciously incompetent in this particular skill set.

Consciously Incompetent

Then as the child starts to grow up and realise what is happening around them, they become very conscious of their incompetence. In their early teenage years they suddenly become aware of the fact that they don't yet know how to drive and that they want to. It is often a struggle for parents to keep eager children calm until the age when they are allowed to start developing their competence in this area and can begin to take driving lessons.

This is true of any new skill set. We discover that there exists some area that we would like to play in, but we realise how little we know. For some people, the vastness of a new modality or field is enough to put them off. They turn away and claim that they are too old, too old fashioned, too out of practice, too 'something' to learn a new skill set and they remain forever conscious of their incompetence in a field.

Consciously Competent

However, some people press in. Although the field is broad, we want to learn about it. This is a huge learning curve and can be daunting and frustrating.

In our example, the teenager is now taking driving lessons. They need to think about the rules of the road, the mechanics of the car they are driving, and the actions of other road users, all at the same time. For new drivers, this is hugely challenging. They have to make dozens of decisions in a split second and they apply huge amounts of concentration to what they are doing. Other people in the car need to be quiet and still to not distract the driver and that poor driver often wonders if they will ever be able to do it, and wouldn't it just be easier to order an Uber instead, for the rest of their lives.

Unconsciously Competent

Then eventually we get to the fourth stage. The driver now has enough practice in this skill set, that the actions start to come naturally to them. They can handle sudden changes on the road, they can handle the weather, they can handle power outages that make other road users crazy, and they can handle noisy passengers, all while navigating roads and getting everyone home safely. They are unconsciously competent in this skill set.

Reflective Competence

A fifth level has been suggested, that of Reflective Competence. This allows us to look at our own unconscious competence, but be able to identify the models, assumptions, and path we took to get there so that we can guide others to their new levels of competence.

How to use this 4 Stages of Learning Model

When we spend enough time getting good at our skills, we become unconsciously competent. That is not a bad place to be. We need to be there to do a good job and to offer value. But we need to challenge ourselves to not stay there all the time.

The Fifth Stage of Reflective Competence is vital when we act as thought leaders. We cannot assume that everyone has the same foundation of knowledge as ourselves, and we cannot solve problems if we are not reflecting on this stage further.

We can also dip back into Conscious Competence, the Third Stage, from time to time. This slowing down and becoming conscious again of each stage, is important when we need to teach someone else the steps involved.

As we teach a new driver how to manage the car and the road and the rules, we become very conscious of each step that we have taken for granted. It is essential, in order to teach and it is important for us to evaluate our own performance.

Think about what happens when you are teaching someone else in your area of speciality. You have spent years learning your craft and internalising the skills, values, and ecosystem of your world. For you it is like breathing; it is unconscious.

You will need to slow down enough to articulate each step to someone new, perhaps a student, or an audience, or someone reading your instruction manual. You are at Stage 5 in your mindset, operating at Stage 4 in your actions, and slowing down to Stage 3 in your instructions. But your audience has just arrived at Stage 2. They have only just accepted that they are utterly incompetent at what already excel at. And for them, it is a scary and overwhelming place to be. What you naturally live and breathe, is for them insurmountable and next to impossible.

That is how we apply our consciousness of being conscious, to the learning process. Let us look at a few other places where consciousness is demonstrating its value before we return to the conversation of being a conscious futurist.

Conscious Leadership

Conscious leadership is a concept that has overturned traditional leadership training.

Starting with 15 Commitments, Conscious Leadership has us think about our intentions of leadership in a new way. In the past, authoritarian, dictatorial leadership might have been acceptable, but it no longer is. Conscious Leadership means that we reject drama, take responsibility and embrace integrity and appreciation and seek resolutions that are wins for everyone instead of just for the benefit of the leader and the organisation.

A Conscious Leader knows that he is not telling people how to do something, but rather creating an environment where everybody can add their wisdom, their insight, and their collective knowledge and mastery of the topic at hand. That's the magic, that is the alchemy that we have when we put our egos aside and intentionally co-create something that will be better than any of us could have done on our own. A conscious leader allows us to do that.

Conscious Consumption

Now that we can lead with conscious intention, it is time to think about how we consume. Conscious Consumption is a movement designed to help us become increasingly aware of the origin and nature of what we consume, as well as how media and advertising is designed to encourage consumption in a way that we might not otherwise have chosen.

The opposite of retail therapy, consuming consciously means that we are aware that our financial choices have an impact on more than our bank balance and potentially our waistline. Way back in 1954, James Buchanan explained how our purchasing power was the truest form of democracy. We vote with our money. We indicate approval or disapproval, by how we spend. Or if not approval, at least that we condone the value chain that produced the article or service we are purchasing.

While many people dismiss the activism that is inherent in conscious consumption, there is plenty of evidence that stakeholders pay attention. Beyond consumer groups, the impact of people refusing to purchase, or switching their purchasing decisions based on the ethical characteristics of the producers, means that companies do respond. Workplace culture, the age, and care of workers, sustainability guidelines, value chain ethics, the care and concern of people, planet, profits as well as purpose, all have an effect on conscious consumers 'choices and ultimately on how the producers produce.

Conscious Capitalism

And that brings us to Conscious Capitalism.

The Conscious Capitalism Credo starts with an assertion that the principle of capitalism is sound, but it is executed poorly. A conscious approach to this economic system can produce better results. The Credo starts:

"We believe that business is good because it creates value, it is ethical because it is based on voluntary exchange, it is noble because it can elevate our existence, and it is heroic because it lifts people out of poverty and creates prosperity.... But we can aspire to even more."

This approach embraces the Quadruple Bottom Line: business should care about People, Planet, Profit, and Purpose.

The first three P's of the traditional Triple Bottom Line; people, planet, and profit, are not just spreadsheet entries to balance up to avoid getting bad PR. They are intended to make us aware of, conscious of sustainability goals and to examine companies 'social, environmental, and economic impact. Actually, I don't know that we can call a 25-year-old framework 'traditional'. The sustainability advisor, John Elkington, who coined the phrase 'Triple Bottom Line 'is frustrated at it being used to measure profit and loss instead of being used to guide businesses to make better sustainably-aware decisions.

So perhaps that is why the addition of 'Purpose 'to that list is so powerful. If a company is true to a truly aspirant purpose, then it is so much easier to make difficult decisions that are not based purely on financial returns.

An example of a response to the concept of conscious business/corporations/capitalism is a new type of organisation called a 'B-corp 'or 'benefit corporation'. These organisations exist knowing that they serve a higher purpose than only to make the shareholders wealthy.

B Corp companies claim that their status and dedication to their mission means that they:
- Attract the best talent and reduce staff turnovers
- Attract impact investment from dedicated fund managers
- Stay ahead of policy and public opinion changes with respect to good practice and sustainability issues
- Get good media exposure and free PR
- Develop a valuable brand image

What else can we be conscious about?

If consciousness is being aware of and paying attention to, then we should be conscious about everything worth doing. We can explore the philosophy and the expression of that philosophy, in areas such as education, architecture, botany, and medicine. What about conscious law and conscious HR practices and conscious energy production, science, cities or art and sport?

There are endless fields where we can apply a consciousness mindset. All it requires is that we start with paying a little more attention to why we are doing what we are doing, choosing, and encountering.

Now we are ready to explore becoming conscious futurists.

#4 The Conscious Futurist Spiral

When we think of motivation models we often imagine examples that are reflected in stages, steps, or levels. For example, Maslow's Hierarchy of Needs is a staged approach where we need to satisfy one need before we can move onto the next.

We know that isn't a good reflection of reality. We do not wait until one part of our lives is exactly right, before starting to develop the next part.

That is why a spiral works well to picture how we think about the future. The spiral is constantly revolving and we, messy humans that we are, are sliding up and sliding down that spiral all the time. We are not consistent nor are we constant. We do not achieve a stage and stop and celebrate and then gather our resources and strength to get up to the next stage. We are not on the next rung, leaving lower rungs behind. We could be more evolved in our thinking in one part of our lives, but be at a very different level in another part, at the same time.

With a spiral, we can be moving up or down all the time. We cannot reach a plateau and just relax there for a little while because if you relax on a spiral, you're just going to start slipping down again. The nice thing about a spiral is that if we do start to slip down, as long as we can recall that we have been at a higher level before, then we know that we can get back up there again. We have that memory of how we used to be and we can achieve that level of thinking again.

It is not that hard. We can inch our way up. We can take a very slow journey moving up the spiral. It does not need to be a huge effort like with steps or stages, where we have to expend a big effort to change our position. The spiral is a different way of looking at progress in terms of futures thinking. It is about our mindset. Let us look at what these five parts are in terms of the *Conscious Futurist Spiral*.

Survival

The first ring right at the bottom is Survival. I challenge anybody in this pandemic world to tell me that they haven't slipped all the way down the spiral to survival level at some stage in the worst of the global crisis.

People have said that the word 'survival' is very negative and that we should have a more positive word to start with. But it is an honest word and the first thing we need to be when we are being conscious is to be honest with ourselves. We need an honest word like 'survival' because that is very literally what many people have had to experience. We have all had a shared crisis with Covid and while it has inconvenienced some people, it has been immensely traumatic for others. Even if we only talk about the effect of the pandemic on lives, livelihoods, and industries, and don't factor in any our personal dramas, survival is a valid experience for many people.

What do we do in Survival mode? We have to make sure that we are safe. If we think about what many people experienced during the lockdowns and movement control orders around the world in response to Covid, we can see how this plays out.

People were told to stay home and that they would only be able to go out in emergencies. Our first thoughts are, are we physically safe? Then, do we have enough food? What about other supplies, medicines at home, internet connection? Are my children, my family, safe in this building for the next few weeks? Do we have enough money in the bank to get us past this weekend, and the next week?

Other crises that bring us to this state include losing a job, getting a serious medical diagnosis, losing money in a bad investment or a scam, losing a loved one, living in a war zone, being repatriated, exiled, or displaced or being personally attacked.

We have to survive as humans before we can explore any other futures issues. The most responsible thing you can do for the future is to survive any crisis you are in. Only after you have survived, can you be responsible.

Responsible

The next ring is to be Responsible. Now we are moving up the spiral.

While we are moving up another ring on the spiral, think about your circle of concern. In the Survival ring, your circle of concern is very tight. It contained your immediate family and probably only a few days or the end of the week in your field of vision.

If we know that our immediate needs are met, that we are okay just for now, then we have the capacity to extend our circle of concern. We can now consider other people like extended family, our close friends, perhaps our employees or team members. Where we are leaders, our teams and staff are of vital importance and it is imperative of our leadership responsibility to ensure that they are alright through a crisis and meet any needs that are appropriate for us to meet. Our timeline also extends a little. Instead of just thinking about how we are going to get through this week, we are now looking at next month.

To become responsible means to intentionally lift yourself from survival, to overcome a tendency to play the victim, and to tart to reclaim your life and your future.

Invested

Invested is the next ring. Now we are moving beyond ourselves and our own immediate concerns and responsibilities.

When we look beyond ourselves to others and toward a further future, we become invested. We are invested in issues to which we have spent a great deal of time or effort developing. Our concern might be for our business, industry, our city, or a club or association to which we belong. We may have a voice in the media or be a social media influencer. It is at this stage that the actions we take and the words we express influence a wider range of people and have an impact over a slightly longer period of time. We invest our efforts in that expanded circle of people and time.

People who spend that time and effort on important issues beyond themselves are Invested Futurists.

Conscious

What comes next is the Conscious Futurist.

We are on the next ring, and our circles of concern are getting bigger in terms of the timeframe and the people.

Now we are not just looking at next year or maybe the year after. Hopefully, we are looking at the next decade. We are not only concerning ourselves with people who know us, but we realise that our choices and actions have an impact on many lives whose names we will never know, and we realise that our actions do not only affect them but also all the lives whom they touch.

Our impact spans years and continents. We will never know

the exact accounting of all that we have impacted or influenced but someone at the Conscious Futurist level does not have an ego that needs to have that accounting.

Conscious Futurists are making culture changes and policy changes. They are investing in and making changes to education and climate. They are thinking about the world that their children's children will be living in. They are looking way beyond the balance sheet, even beyond the triple bottom line, and want to know that their lives are defined by a purpose beyond themselves.

Transcendent

The highest ring on the Conscious Futurist Spiral is that of the Transcendent Futurist.

Now we are going beyond time and place and people. We are declaring a manifesto about what we believe the world could look like. Being transcendent means to move beyond the normal range of physical human experience, or to climb or go beyond.

I am not suggesting that we should necessarily be seeking esoteric ways, but to be a philosophical, transcendent, conscious futurist, means you value something beyond this time frame or this current existence.

Now we are looking at our culture, values, heritage. How are people's lives going to be better, how are cities or organisations going to transform because of our influence? What are we going to pick up or put down, so that way more than just our lives are changed?

Transcendent futurists know that they will never receive the accolades, the awards, the recognition for what they have done. The payoff may only come years after they are gone, and perhaps someone else will get the credit. But this futurist wants more than personal gratification. They want to make a dent in the world, even if most of the world forgets their name.

You can be this Conscious Futurist or Transcendent Futurist

While it is tempting to think that only people with a huge platform or massive influence, can operate at these levels and that we don't have to try beyond being responsible, or maybe invested, it is possible for anyone to have influence at that deep and abiding level.

Being Conscious or Transcendent doesn't mean that you have to touch the lives of millions. It could mean that you touch one life so deeply, that millions are influenced.

Think of any famous person who has made a deep and abiding influence on the lives of millions, down the generations. We wonder who was that person who encouraged, cajoled, celebrated, picked up and dusted off our hero, to help them, who touched their life so that they could touch ours. We don't know the names of the hero behind the hero, but that person was likely a conscious futurist, investing in the life of one to the benefit of many over many years.

How the spiral works, why it isn't a step/lock system

Co-ordinate your levels

As ambitious human souls, of course, we want to keep moving up the Spiral. But it is important to realise that it is okay to slip down from time to time.

We want to transcend, we want to invest our lives and efforts in something meaningful. But something will happen, like an illness or an accident, or some other crisis in our lives, that will pull us down to that bottom level. And that is okay because our first responsibility is to survive. It has to be. We cannot do anything for anyone else if we cannot catch our own breath. We cannot save our families or businesses or rescue clients or colleagues, we cannot impress anybody or pursue ambitions if we cannot survive. Our first responsibility to anybody else is to take care of ourselves.

So have respect for yourself, if you have come down to that level. And don't think of it as any kind of fault or punishment. That's where you have to be at this stage. But remember that if you have been at a higher level before, then you will be able to get back there. You also don't need to rush it. Take your time. We are not in competition with each other.

Also, think about where your audience is. Whether you are talking with staff or family or clients, you need to be aware of where you are on the spiral and you need to work out where they are. Otherwise, the best scenarios for the future will come unstuck if you are operating at different levels and you don't realise it.

If you are at a higher level of futures thinking than your audience, if you can imagine scenarios for the future and you are identifying opportunities, but they are in crisis mode, then they cannot hear you. If you paint pictures of fantastic futures, you could cause them distress rather than helping them through their immediate crisis.

And if you try to do work for people who are at a higher level than you are at the moment, if you are struggling at Survival level and they are casting a huge vision, then you cannot serve them. You will frustrate their plans and their vision may cause you pain until you can start to move back up the Spiral. You can only design a message to land with someone, to really connect, if you understand where you both are in terms of your thinking about the future.

It is okay to be unconscious sometimes

As much as we are talking about being conscious, we have to

know that we cannot be fully conscious all the time about everything. It's exhausting. We will be overwhelmed by sensory input and fatigued by constant decision making. We cannot get through the day without relying on habits, conventions, programs, assumptions, algorithms, patterns in our brains, and our thinking.

We know that websites and computer programs all run on algorithms. Algorithms are set processes or rules that have been established to most efficiently come to the solution to a problem. We think that we humans are not constrained by that type of thinking but the truth is that we operate according to internal algorithms, constantly. Over time we have created mental shortcuts or heuristics, frameworks, to process information and make decisions.

Our goal is not to remove them entirely. That would be painful and cause incredible inefficiencies in our lives. But we do need to challenge them from time to time. We need to be aware of the fact that we have them, and then assess them to see if they fit with our values and are the best processing tools we could use.

There are a few natural times in our lives when we are inclined to stop and assess. If we become ill, are facing surgery, give birth to a child, face a major birthday, experience a year like 2020 when all the rules are broken; these are the times that we naturally become internally focussed and reflective. If these occasions of reflection leave us despondent, then we have a problem. Instead, we could anticipate these times and create a summary of how we have developed since our last reflection, and determine how close we are to the preferred scenario that we have devised.

Because you are a philosophical futurist, you can build new opportunities into your life to do this exercise too. You don't have to wait for a crisis.

Once you have reassessed your path and goals, you can intentionally build in certain shortcuts that you don't need to pay attention to, so that you can free up your mind for more important things like scanning the horizon for changes to your circle of influence. Become ever so slightly unconscious in some areas, knowing that you will re-evaluate them later so that you can be more conscious in new areas that you are exploring.

#5 How Alex Moved Down And Then Back Up The Conscious Futurist Spiral

Alex is a well-established entrepreneur in the events industry. The founder of her own events and conference organiser business, Alex is respected by staff, clients and colleagues, and contributes beyond just the business of her business, by volunteering in her association and mentoring young people coming into the events space.

In terms of the Spiral, Alex could well be placed comfortably at the Conscious Futurist stage. Let us look at a small part of her resume.

Alex's business employs over 90 people, over 6 branches, in 3 countries. She has purchased equipment and invested in physical assets to help to cater for the hundreds of events that the company either organises or provides resources for, on an annual basis. Staff are paid well with decent benefits and the low turnover of employees indicates that the staff are predominately happy with their positions. There are opportunities for employees to learn new skills, change or advance in positions within the company, or occasionally be seconded to other companies to assist with a short-term project, thereby improving their skills, experience, and ultimately, their own CVs.

Beyond the business, Alex serves as on the board of a local in-dustry association, has served a term as both treasurer and then president of an international federation of events organisers, and started a new association to focus on the development of young talent in the conferencing industry. This latter project sees her rally colleagues to volunteer time, skills, money, and other re-sources to deliver a curriculum that has seen almost 150 young people trained and given internships in this exciting space.

Alex's contribution was in people way beyond her own imme-diate circle of family and friends. Her contribution will see divi-dends for many years, even if no one ever came back and shared a story with the person who gave them their start in business, Alex's influence on those lives and careers will ripple through many families, many business, and different parts of the world for years to come. Alex was well and truly making a conscious contri-bution to the future of her industry and her world.

Then COVID-19 happened.

One of the very first industries to be affected by the lockdowns or movement control orders designed to keep people physically distant to prevent the spread of the coronavirus, was any form of event or conference. The events industry came to a sudden and dramatic halt. Overnight calendars of upcoming events were wiped clean, not just locally but around the world. At the same time as people stopped moving because they were restricted to their homes, money stopped moving too. Outstanding proposals were scrapped. Tentative arrangements were cancelled. Obscure legal clauses were used to get out of contracts. Years 'worth of historic data used to predict industry seasons and to plan to scale up activities at certain times of the year for different parts of the world, suddenly became irrelevant.

Alex slid down the Spiral, rapidly. From someone consciously creating opportunities for herself and for others, locally and glo-bally, now and into the future, Alex found herself in the unbeliev-

able position of being in Survival mode.

For almost a week, Alex took to bed. She hid under the duvet and slept fretfully to try to avoid processing the implications of a global halt to business, with no end in sight and no clear official views on when, if ever, things might get back to what once was normal.

On the rare occasions in that first week that Alex got out of bed, her only concern was for her family at home. Did they have what they needed? Was there enough food or would someone have to leave the house, and perhaps answer to police about where they were going? How could she and her husband explain this bizarre concept to their children, who had been raised to believe that they lived in a relatively free world? How were the children going to learn if they couldn't go to school? Was school cancelled only for a short while or would they have to make other plans in the future? Was it only for 3 weeks that they would be stuck at home or might that last longer? What if there was a medical emergency that had nothing to do with COVID? Could they go to the doctor? Did they have enough money in their bank account to cover payments and the house payments? Was it too soon to go back to bed and sleep some more?

Everyone deserves a duvet day from time to time, and after a few in a row, and once the sheer panic of the situation had calmed down in Alex's mind and stomach, she took a deep breath and started looking beyond.

Beyond her family, safe at home, with food and enough entertainment to keep the children occupied, beyond them, were other people that Alex cared about. In the second week of lockdown, Alex started reaching out to family, to her parents and siblings, to close friends. The short check-ins were sometimes light-hearted, sometimes extraordinarily difficult. Managing her own emotions while trying to encourage someone else was so draining that Alex often needed time and a distraction to try to re-distance herself from other peoples 'trauma before her empathy had a chance to destroy her.

But her extended family were not the only people Alex was Responsible for. Getting in touch with the management team, online, in the second week of homestay, Alex and the team started to make plans that they knew would evolve, change, perhaps become null and void, even as local government and international bodies kept changing their positions on what could or could not be done to live in a world with a global pandemic. Never before had Alex realised just how much of adult life is made up on the spot, as people try to be resourceful in changing circumstances. There was no definitive guidebook to this situation. They really had to rely on their own judgements.

Alex and her team started to make plans for their employees of the business. There were different rules in the three different countries over which her business extended. Some of the governments already were offering some employee assistance in terms of supporting lost salaries. There were government schemes, banking schemes, and advisory groups which were already coming out with plans, products, and services to assist those in this crisis. The company management team had to decide if they were going to and if they could afford to, continue paying salaries, or if they had to be reduced. They made a difficult decision, that if the situation were to extend longer than just a few weeks, that they would reduce all salaries in the company, on a sliding scale of the more senior people taking a bigger pay cut, than those on smaller packages already.

After discussing legal issues, HR issues, marketing responses, the safety of their physical assets while no one was around, after making a hundred decisions in a day or two, Alex was again exhausted. Exhausted but encouraged. She had a good team, and while they were struggling with everything that was going on, they were determined to do the best they could for each other, and for any clients who still needed their services. She knew that her staff were suffering, and not every day went smoothly as emotions erupted out of anxiety for the implications of an uncertain future, but all they could do was support each other and try to find the best solutions for each individual.

A few weeks passed and turned into months, and along with the rest of the world, it started to become apparent to Alex, that firstly, the virus wasn't just going to disappear but that it was going to be a real part of everyday life for a long time to come. And secondly, there was no going back to how things used to be, probably ever. So many businesses and organisations had already failed which meant that around the world, thousands upon thousands of people were having to redefine what it was they did for a living. They were learning new ways of working, of living, of creating value, and of course, of earning an income. When the people change, the businesses have to change too and that means that industries and sectors would have to adjust in many ways. As would the events industry. What that looked like, Alex did not yet know but as the president of her local association, she was invited to join an industry collaborative to discuss exactly that.

For the first time in her memory, she saw associations get together and share insights, knowledge, resources and support to find out how their sector was going to survive. The associations in the collaborative represented the different facets of events, conferencing, exhibitions, and related fields. The work they did was varied and not everything was effective, but they were learning as they meet weekly to address issues collectively. They engaged with media to explain what the industry was doing for workers as well as how events might be handled safely, had occasional meetings with relevant government officials to discuss initiatives that would help them, and found ways to support and provide resources to each other, each others 'members and the large community of people around their work.

Alex started wondering what they might also be able to do

once things had settled down from Covid. She didn't imagine that the current problems would disappear and she was heartbroken as she watched colleagues 'businesses falter and fail. But after she took a deep breath, she turned her attention to the future. Individually, some of the associations had internships, youth outreach, or education programmes but perhaps they could do something collectively. Perhaps they could jointly fund or support a comprehensive programme to allow new people into the industry to learn a range of skills across their different areas. There could a national certificate issued and a joint gala. This was going to be fun; not today, but one day soon. Alex was invested again!

The next few months saw everyone continuously adjusting, reinventing, reassessing, prioritising. People were pivoting like ballerinas. New words were used, abandoned, and then used again when nothing else made sense. They really did need to be agile. They really did have to work out what the new normal would look like.

For Alex, some very difficult decisions needed to be made about her business. Some staff left because they could use their skills in other areas where they could be employed at a full salary. Tragically, two members of Alex's staff contracted Covid and passed away, while a few others thankfully recovered. She had to close down one office after struggling to keep it open. But the concern and anxiety over her now-former employees 'welfare in that office, caused her no relief at finally making that decision.

The business was totally reorganised. Staff worked from home as much as possible, and the leases on unnecessary office space were allowed to lapse. Contracts with both suppliers and clients were renegotiated, but with the intention of supporting each others 'business during this time rather than trying to squeeze out every little bit of potential profit. Alex asked her colleagues in the broader industry to help some of her staff with a little coaching or training, at negotiated prices, so that those staff members could have some chance of finding a better chance at full employment.

Alex started conversations with colleagues in other parts of the world. At first, it was just to connect with friends she hadn't been able to see at their annual conventions, but eventually, they turned into a series of small mastermind sessions, jointly looking for responses to their experiences in their own part of the world and sharing research and reports that could add insight and perhaps generate some creative solutions.

It was out of those international conversations that a new idea for events was born. Alex started a project in her business to provide the sorts of resources she used to for physical meetings, but now in the virtual space. Where she used to provide room decor, her team now designed fun, relevant, and helpful virtual backgrounds, some in video format. Where she used to provide AV equipment to large conferences, she now sourced, sold, or rented AV equipment for home offices. She set up both a training division and a team that would go and install home-based video conferencing for the staff and management of companies who needed professional help to provide an excellent online experience. She and her team attended every session they could, researched, experimented, consulted, and practiced, until they became exceptionally adept at hosting really good, interesting, interactive, and valuable online sessions. They then taught others, earning a reputation for delivering exceptional training and becoming sought-after experts. While this was developing, Alex set up a full curriculum of what they had learned and what they were teaching and started to replicate these experiences in other parts of the world, developing a team of contracted professional virtual facilitators who delivered both her material as well as their own. Those independent contractors, while not officially on her payroll, were certainly earning more than they had before she connected with them and gave them an opportunity to develop this skill.

The business began to evolve, moving away slightly from the physical space and developing rapidly in the virtual space. While Alex had had to close three offices eventually, she now had numerous representatives in 15 different countries. She noticed how demand for those facilitators often rose dramatically as that country went into a second or third wave of Covid cases, but the income from different parts of the world meant that she was not at the mercy of what was happening locally.

She also started donating some of her staff's time to help other organisations that were not as quick or well resourced, to respond to the online world. The staff loved the idea and a flurry of organisations, schools, charities, and causes were added to a long list of people that they wanted to volunteer their time and services to. Alex worried a little that they might be diluting their business focus with this, but after seeing the enthusiasm for the project, she agreed to a bold plan. Every staff member would be allowed to donate one day a week to serving a charity-type project, with the work they do. They consulted, coached, trained, and occasionally pitched in some funds to buy equipment for those causes that were close to their hearts. Alex's colleagues warned her that she was seriously undercutting her profits, but she persevered with the project, to which she had agreed to a 6-month trial. Something was evolving but she couldn't quite name it yet.

Then one day one of the independent contractors in another country, contacted Alex and explained that they had heard what her staff at home were doing and that they wanted to do something similar. He had been in touch with a few other of her contractors, and they wanted to volunteer their own time to use the company's resources and material in a similar way. After a little negotiation, almost 90% of the contractors agreed to a different pay structure on the basis that they would be partially compensated for the time they spent training charities and schools on Alex's methodologies.

Productivity went through the roof. The staff were so engaged at intentionally creating a better world for their own causes and colleagues, that they worked harder and better at regular work to ensure enough income to support their charitable efforts. The clients loved the idea when they heard about it, and some of them came forward to offer their own resources from time to time, to bolster the efforts of Alex's staff. Of course, the media found out eventually and the press coverage was incredible, the more so because Alex had never sought it so the efforts of her staff were not seen as a PR stunt.

Far from losing 20% of revenue because the staff donated one day a week to charity, the company's income rose steadily. The engaged staff became more creative about how they responded to the continuing challenges of Covid, as well as to other occasional challenges that disrupted their plans. They became more resourceful, more confident and business started pouring in from new sectors that Alex had never considered pursuing. She hadn't yet recovered financially from the early months of devastation on her business, but she was happier with her work than she had ever been before.

When asked what she felt about the future now, Alex answered that she was consciously co-creating a future with her staff. It was going to be amazing. It was already amazing.

On reflection later Alex wondered that if everything she was doing had seemed impossible just a few months back, but was now evolving naturally into the amazing experience it was, then she wondered what else might be possible. How could she develop something in this space that would add value to more people, further away, and perhaps for many more years down the line? She wondered if she could now be more than just conscious of the future she was creating. Could she, in fact, transcend the expectations and limitations she had had about her own life and create something that would, she struggled for a word. Could it be even better? Could she create something even more than she currently thought possible. She thought that she just might be able to do that.

#6 HOW TO DEVELOP TO MOVE UP THE SPIRAL

Right, so we want to move up the Spiral. We want to become more Conscious Futurists. How do we do that?

Experiment with some of the ideas on this list to see what might work for you.

Explore beyond your circle

We know that our social media feeds are echo chambers of people saying what we already believe and agree with. We naturally tend towards following content that fits with our established beliefs. So very quickly we begin to see the world as a reflection of ourselves, and then we are stunned to discover that other people, some whom we respect, have fundamentally different views from what we believe is the norm.

To ensure that you are not stunned too often, or stunned in a way that becomes unhelpful, regularly expose yourself to other views by seeking them out. They aren't going to come to you.

Scanning is a good futures thinking tool. Scanning means you become aware of, pay some attention to, but don't have to become an expert in, a concept that is new to you. Scan social media, news feeds, videos, newspapers, reports, infographics, from places you don't normally go. It might mean you start paying attention to the news headlines of a different region of the world. Or perhaps you subscribe to an interesting newsletter from an industry that is not naturally related to your own. Sign up for free webinars from other associations or companies and see what they are doing.

What will you learn? Different approaches to similar problems. Deep concerns about issues you were not aware of. Values and assumptions about life, love, and relationships that surprise you. Essentially, you will become less assured that your way of life is the only way, the most natural way. Hopefully, it makes you more open-minded and curious and able to engage people with different ideas, so that together you can co-create new approaches.

Play with opposite ideas

Another way to seriously challenge your unexamined pre-conceptions is to do comparative reading. Play with opposite ideas. If you are subscribed to a news site with a clear political leaning, then find their opposite and read their headlines at the same time. It is scary to discover how easily a set of facts can be spun to suit an agenda. If you have religious beliefs, then read the original stories of another religion and compare. See how the religions or divisions evolved and how each side tells the story in a way that fits with their narrative. If you are looking for dieting advice, personal development, how to build a mailing list, then look for people with different modalities and a different focus. You will learn that some people who dogmatically declare that their way is the only way that works miss out on some incredibly valuable tools and insights that some other practitioner may offer. Don't get stuck with the first version of what you learn, not if you want to be conscious about the future you create.

Consider the passage of time

Time is what prevents everything from happening at once. But how we view time affects how we live now and how we plan for the future. Back in 2019, many organisations would have made ambitious plans for their next five years, hoping to help their members or staff and their clients to evolve and embrace new technologies. Within a few weeks of the start of 2020, although some companies had collapsed, many others found that those long-term goals transformational goals were reached. Overnight our industries adapted and changed. But other things will need to be invested in over time and the results won't be seen for years. We either become impatient or despondent over how much time it takes to achieve our development goals.

Spend time, invest time perhaps, in philosophically contemplating the passage of time. And know that your agenda might not be at the same pace as someone else's.

Get to grips with your values

If you want to be conscious about the future and the world that we create, then you have to understand what you value. Just by putting something near the top of your list of values, you begin to choose projects and make decisions based on them. You will stay closer to your own conscious path that way, and avoid wasting energy on things that others might prize but which are less important in your internal ledger.

Whether you intuitively know your values, or whether you need to spend time intentionally working out what you prize most in life, being able to name your values creates so much clarity in your life.

Taking the time to reflect upon and define your values means that you create an intentional shortcut in your thinking. It makes you more efficient in decision making and using your energy when your life is aligned with your values framework. However, you do need to build in opportunities to periodically reevaluate them.

As a futurist, I believe that we do all have agency over our lives and our futures. And while of course things will happen that will disrupt our plans, and of course we are members of societies and we need to comply with a certain amount of rules to live in harmony, there is so much that we could be doing to influence the future in the direction that we want to go in.

We need to have the courage and the conviction that as futurists, we have agency over the future, that together, we co-create that future. That is why this conversation is so important.

Insert Life Milestones into your calendar

We must find ways to interrupt our unconscious, knee-jerk response to our lives and insert proactive opportunities to re-imagine how we live.

Apart from those big birthdays, put other opportunities into your calendar that will give you pause to reflect. Many cultures have demonstrated the value of rituals and annual celebrations of important historic events. You could start your own pre-celebration of a place you want to be in your life, or a characteristic you want to develop, or a career goal that you are working towards. Once you have something in mind that you want to work towards in your future, find ways to insert that into your calendar so that on a particular day each year, or a regular time each quarter, you stop to contemplate how far you have come towards your goal and celebrate it and reinforce why you are working towards it. It will always be a journey, not a destination, but we have pauses on journeys to get some rest, to check our route, to renew our commitment to the path we are on.

Your own ideas

My highest value is that of agency. I believe people should have the freedom to make their own decisions (within the shared responsibility of being part of a well-functioning society). So take this list above as only the start of your own list of ways to think about the future and become a more conscious futurist. Then develop your own ways.

The future is in your hands. Make it a good one.

Afterword

This book is a summary of a keynote presentation I have done many times in the last year. Should you wish to discuss how this topic might be of value to your association members or your organisational team, please be in touch.

Coupled with a presentation called 'Futures Literacy - The Professional Development Skill we are Missing' these presentations help organisations to begin to embrace the skills of futures thinking to prepare their organisations for whatever changes come their way.

The author can be found at the following places.

www.charlottekemp.co.za
alchemist@charlottekemp.co.za
www.linkedin.com/in/charlottekemp

About The Author

Charlotte Kemp

Charlotte Kemp is the Futures Alchemist, a futurist keynote speaker who works with organisations to co-create preferred futures.

Charlotte is a member of the Association of Professional Futurists (APF) and holds leadership positions in the Professional Speakers Association of Southern Africa (PSASA) and the Global Speakers Federation (GSF).

Charlotte is also the author of a number of books, including 'Futures Alchemist' which presents a narrative of how to use her Map, Compass and Guide model to navigate unknown futures.

For research and insight, Charlotte hosts a podcast series called 'Futures Facets' and interviews people around the world to gain an understanding of how we see the future from our different points of view.